I0626418

Written by Jessica Tyrrell MSN, BSN, RN
Edited by Abbey McLaughlin
Cover designed by GetCovers
Published by Dynamic Content Solutions LLC

DYNAMIC
CONTENT SOLUTIONS

Disclaimer

This book is intended solely for educational and informational purposes. The content provided herein does not constitute medical, nursing, pharmaceutical, or other professional healthcare advice, diagnosis, or treatment. Readers should not use the information in this book as a substitute for professional medical advice, diagnosis, or treatment from a qualified healthcare provider. Always seek the advice of your physician, pharmacist, or other qualified healthcare professional with any questions you may have regarding a medical condition, medication, or treatment. Never disregard professional medical advice or delay seeking it because of something you have read in this book. Do not use this book in medical emergencies. In the event of an emergency, call your baby's pediatrician or 911 immediately.

Use of the information in this book is entirely at your own risk. The authors, editors, and publishers of this book expressly disclaim any responsibility or liability for any adverse effects, loss, injury, or damage incurred as a direct or indirect result of the use or application of any information contained in this book. Although the author has attempted to confirm the accuracy of the information in this book as of the date of publication, the author, editors, and publishers do not make any representations, warranties, or guarantees of any kind as to the correctness or accuracy of the information in this book. Additionally, medical information changes rapidly and therefore, some information in this book may be out of date at the time readers use the information in this book.

The mention of specific products, procedures, or therapies does not constitute an endorsement or recommendation by the authors, editors, or publishers. The authors, editors, and publishers do not represent or warrant that any particular product, procedure, or therapy is safe, appropriate, or effective for you or your baby under any particular circumstances, conditions, or criteria. And, in no event shall the authors, editors, or publishers be liable for any.

The medication dosing mentioned in this book is a generic dosing table for common medications used in this population. All medication dosing should be checked for manufacturer dosing and your pediatrician's weight-based dosing. Additionally, dosage recommendations may vary based on individual factors, including age, weight, medical history, and the presence of other conditions or medications. Always double-check medicine concentrations as like medications may be different. Readers should consult a licensed healthcare provider before adopting or changing medication regimens to ensure individual safety and the effectiveness of treatment. Medications can interact with other drugs, underlying health conditions, and individual characteristics such as age, weight, and medical history. Only a licensed healthcare provider has the training and expertise to evaluate these factors and determine the most appropriate course of action for each individual.

Inspired by:

Rett, Hank & Caroline

"The sniffles and cries won't last too long, though the nights feel tough, and the days feel wrong. The season is tough, but it soon slips away--- And you'll miss those snuggles one ordinary day."

-Unknown

TABLE OF CONTENTS

Medicine Cabinet

At some point, your baby will get sick. This is meant to be a quick reference book to help you and your baby through it! The first step to getting through it is to be prepared for it. A well-stocked house should include the following:

Children's Acetaminophen

Acetaminophen suppositories

Children's Ibuprofen

*Be Aware: Children's Ibuprofen is sold in two concentrations: Infant's drops (50mg/1.25mL) or Children's liquid (100mg/5mL).

Gripe Water

Simethicone/Infant Gas Relief Drops

Saline Spray

Teething Gel/Teething Drops

Diphenhydramine (Benadryl®)

Vapor Rub

Electrolyte Solution

Thermometer

Nose Sucker (Bulb Syringe, Oral-Nasal Aspirator, Electric Aspirator)

Saline Nose Spray or Drops

Nose Picker

Medicine Pacifier or Oral Syringes with Pre-Marked Dosing

Fever

The rectal temperature is the most accurate in infants aged 0-1 years.

Axillary (armpit), ear and temporal (forehead) thermometers are often 0.5-1 degree lower than rectal temperature.

Oral temperature should not be attempted on infants aged 0-1.

What Temperature Is a Fever?

Newborn to three months: 100.4 °F / 38.0 °C

Three months and older: 102 °F / 38.9 °C

Contact pediatrician for any fever in a baby three months of age and younger.

Tips on Taking Temperature:

For rectal temperature, use small amount of lubrication on tip of thermometer. Have baby on back in diaper-changing position and hold legs up or have a helper hold baby over shoulder, held snuggly, and insert tip approximately ½ an inch to 1 inch into rectum.

You can keep diaper on when checking rectal temperature—just loosen and pull it to the side. Baby may have a bowel movement afterward from the rectal stimulation.

Many companies make rectal thermometers with shorter tips to take the guessing out of how far to insert the tip.

For armpit temperature, hold the thermometer in place and give baby a "hug" to keep the arms down. Make sure the temperature probe doesn't extend out past the armpit.

Fever Reduction Strategies:

There are a couple of important things to note when treating your infant for a fever. Infants under the age of 6 months old should not have Ibuprofen. Acetaminophen is the recommended medication to treat a fever. Contact your pediatrician for any medication dosing under the age of 2 months.

Many infant medications use the same active ingredient across multiple brand labels and formulation types. Always confirm **ingredient**, **concentration**, **age/weight suitability**.

Things You Can Try To Keep Your Febrile Infant Comfortable:

- Dress in light-breathable clothing, avoid bundling up,
- Give them a lukewarm bath or sponge bath (85–90 °F/29–32 °C).
- Avoid cold baths or temperatures, this could increase shivering and increase internal temperature.
- Offer plenty of fluids to keep them hydrated.
- Encourage rest, *Nona says rest is the best medicine!*

Alternating for Fever Reduction:

Alternating Acetaminophen and Ibuprofen for fever reduction is an option when one medication is not effectively reducing your child's fever. This is done by rotating between two medications every 3-4 hours. Ask your pediatrician before trying this method. Do not alternate longer than twenty-four hours. Do not exceed the maximum dosage listed on each medicine bottle in 24 hours. This is not a strategy to use with infants under six months of age, as Ibuprofen should not be given to this age group.

Alternation Dosing Example:

6 a.m. Acetaminophen

9 a.m. Ibuprofen

12 p.m. Acetaminophen

3 p.m. Ibuprofen

Common Fever Medicine Dosing

Infant Ibuprofen Dosing (50mg/1.25mL)

Ibuprofen should not be given to infants under 6 months of age.

Weight	Dose
6-11 lbs	Do not give
12-17 lbs	1.25mL
18-23 lbs	1.875mL
24-35 lbs	2.5mL

Children's Ibuprofen Dosing (100mg/5mL)

Weight	Dose
6-11 lbs	Do not give
12-17 lbs	2.5mL
18-23 lbs	4mL
24-35 lbs	5mL

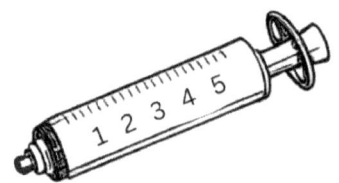

Infants & Children's Acetaminophen Dosing (160mg/5mL)

(They are the same concentration, so you can use for either age. You get more for your money with the Children's Acetaminophen. The infant's packaging comes with a syringe and the children's packaging comes with a medicine cup.)

Weight	Dose
6-11 lbs	1.25mL
12-17 lbs	2.5mL
18-23 lbs	3.75mL
24-35 lbs	5mL

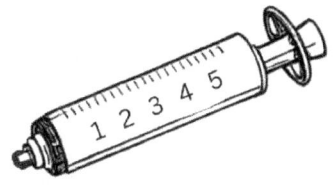

Tips on Medication Administration:

Always keep baby upright when giving medicine. Do not give while they are lying flat.

Using a medicine-pacifier attachment allows the medication to pass through a pacifier adapter to allow the baby to suck and swallow the medication. Check to make sure the medicine hole on pacifier attachment are pointed toward the sides of cheeks.

If using a medicine syringe, point the syringe inside the cheek pocket and slowly push in. You can gently blow in babies face to encourage them to swallow.

You can try mixing it with breastmilk/formula to dilute taste, but use a smaller amount than the infant's normal bottle incase baby doesn't finish a whole bottle, you won't risk them not getting a full dose. Ex: If baby normally drinks 4 oz at a time, only mix with 1-2 oz. This can also be done with juice with older children.

Do not use household teaspoons or tablespoons to measure medication dosages; these are not an accurate method of measurement, and you could risk overdosing the infant.

Always keep track of times and dosages of medicine given so you can refer back to accurate time dosing.

When to contact your pediatrician for a fever:

- For any fever in a baby 3 months old or younger
- Fever lasting more than 2 days
- Signs of dehydration (no wet diapers in four to six hours, inside of lips are dry and tacky, no tears when crying, lethargy)
- Unusual drowsiness or irritability
- Unusual rash

The medication dosing mentioned in this book is a generic dosing table for common medications used in this population. All medication dosing should be checked for manufacturer dosing and your pediatrician's weight-based dosing. Additionally, dosage recommendations may vary based on individual factors, including age, weight, medical history, and the presence of other conditions or medications. Always double-check medicine concentrations as like medications may be different.
Readers should consult a licensed healthcare provider before adopting or changing medication regimens to ensure individual safety and the effectiveness of treatment. Medications can interact with other drugs, underlying health conditions, and individual characteristics such as age, weight, and medical history. Only a licensed healthcare provider has the training and expertise to evaluate these factors and determine the most appropriate course of action for each individual.

Gassy Baby

Digestion starts to mature in babies around three weeks of age. You may start to notice more spit up, fussing, and gas.

Burp your baby often during feedings (every couple ounces, or between switching breasts if breastfeeding) and keep them upright to prevent reflux.

If breastfeeding, certain foods you eat can make baby gassier. If formula feeding, certain formulas can cause more GI upset than others, so talk to your pediatrician about which ones to try.

Things You Can Try for a Gassy Baby:

- Bicycle legs
- Belly massages: massage belly in an upside-down U shape

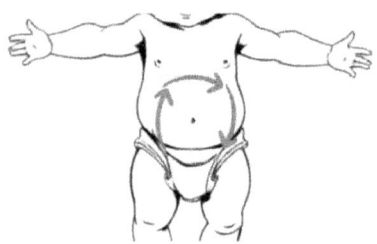

- Warm compresses on the tummy
- Football hold
- Use anti-reflux bottles to prevent the amount of air baby gets during feeds
- Gripe Water: this is a non-pharmacological blend of sodium-bicarb and herbs to help sooth baby's belly
- Gas Drops (Simethicone): medicine used to help break up gas bubbles

Reflux

Reflux often begins around three weeks old, peaks around four to five months, and improves when baby begins to sit up independently and move around on their own.

Most babies spit up milk during burping or after feeding. It isn't considered a problem if they are seemingly content, feed well, and are gaining proper weight. It is also often confused with vomiting, but vomiting is more forceful and of larger amounts.

Reflux May Look Like:

- Arching back
- Fussing during feedings or refusing to eat
- Consistently spitting up large amounts
- Irritable after feeds
- Poor or no weight gain

Contact your pediatrician if your baby shows any of the symptoms from above.

Things You Can Try for Reflux:

- Keep baby upright during and for twenty minutes after feedings
- Burp baby often throughout feed
- Offer smaller amounts in each sitting more frequently throughout the day
- Paced bottle feeding technique
- Anti-colic bottles, which are designed to reduce the amount of air that baby can swallow during feeds

Teething

Can start as early as three months or as late as a year.

Teething May Look Like:

- Irritability
- Gum swelling
- Rosy cheeks
- Excessive drooling
- Chewing or gnawing
- Mild fever
- Ear pulling
- Sleep interruption

Some infants will show teething signs days to weeks before a tooth actually cuts skin, and typically once the tooth breaks skin, their pain is relieved.

Things You Can Try for Teething:

- Cold teethers
- Frozen, wet wash cloths
- Gently rub gums with clean fingers
- Frozen fruit in a silicone or mesh feeder for them to gnaw on
- Infant teething gels
- Freezing water, formula, or breastmilk in the nipple of a bottle. Attach to bottle once frozen and let baby suck/chew on
- Teething crackers if baby is old enough for solids
- Acetaminophen or Ibuprofen if very irritable or interrupting sleep
- Keep cheeks and chin dry as possible (plenty of bibs). The excessive drool can cause a rash. The excessive swallowing of drool can also cause an upset stomach, which can cause frequent, loose stools
- *Nona's tip: Tie a washcloth in a knot, wet it and freeze it. Let baby gum/chew on it.*

Ear Infections

Ear infection symptoms can mimic teething symptoms, and it is difficult to tell them apart.

Ear Infections May Look Like:

- Ear pulling
- Crying when laid flat
- Sleep disruption
- Irritability
- Fluid draining from ear
- Fever
- Loss of balance

You can use over-the-counter medication for pain control. Try to keep baby upright as much as possible to prevent the pressure change of lying down (feeding, diapering, naps).

Signs to Contact Pediatrician:

- If symptoms do not resolve in two to three days
- If blood or pus is seen from ear
- If baby refuses to eat
- If symptoms aren't relieved with over-the-counter medication
- If baby is very uncomfortable

17

Common Cold

The common cold often presents with congestion, runny nose, sneezing, coughing, irritability, and fever.

If a baby younger than three months old shows signs of a cold, especially a fever, call your pediatrician.

Babies are nose breathers until about 3-4 months of age, which makes it very difficult for them to get comfortable if their nose become congested.

Things You Can Try for Nasal Congestion:

- Infant saline spray helps break up mucous and makes it easier to remove.
- Nasal Aspirator Options: bulb syringe, oral-nose aspirator, or electric aspirator. Do this before bottling to make it easier on the baby (babies breathe through their nose when bottling).
- Use bathroom as a steam room. Turn shower on hot and let it run and fill room with steam. Stay in bathroom for five to ten minutes to help break up mucous.
- Use a cool mist humidifier to keep the room moist. Don't use humidifier drops unless your humidifier is able to be taken apart and cleaned.
- Vapor rub on chest, back, and feet.
- *Nona's Tip: Cut up an onion and leave it next to their bed (out of reach). Nona says it helps relieve congestion and allows your little one to get a better night's rest.*

Severe Respiratory Symptoms to Seek Urgent Care:
- Wheezing (look up a video of the noise if you don't know it)
- Stridor noise (tight sounding) made on inhale
- Breathing faster than sixty breaths per minute
  - Shortness of breath
  - Chest sinking in when breathing, area between ribs or above collar bone sucking in when breathing (Look up "retractions" for video of examples)
  - Nostrils flaring
  - Symptoms last longer than ten days

Croup

Croup is commonly caused by a virus that causes swelling of the airways, causing a "barking" cough. (Look up this sound; it is very distinct.) Croup usually begins with common cold symptoms and progresses to a barking cough that becomes worse with crying and coughing, creating a cycle of worsening symptoms. Symptoms are usually worse at night

Symptoms:
- Cold symptoms, Fever
- Distinct "barking cough", hoarse or loss of voice
- Stridor
- Breathing fast, or noisy breathing

Your doctor can prescribe a steroid to reduce the airway swelling. They will likely still have any cold symptoms.

Things You Can Try for Croup:
- Stay calm and try keeping your baby calm to avoid causing crying and coughing fits.
- Have baby breath in cold air, bring them outside, or hold them in the freezer door (dressing them appropriately).
- Keep them hydrated; treat fevers if they occur.
- Any of the nasal congestion tips from the common cold section.

Croup typically sounds worse than it is, but don't hesitate to take them in right away for treatment when you hear the distinct barking cough.

Constipation

Hard, pebble-like stools that are painful for baby to pass.

Things You Can Try for Constipation:

- Babies one month and older may have small amounts of water throughout the day (ask pediatrician how much they recommend).
- You can add an ounce of juice in the morning and afternoon with pediatrician approval to help naturally soften stools (pear, prune, or white grape juice made for babies).
- Rectal stimulation with a rectal thermometer (look up how to do this safely).
- Babies four months or older may eat foods such as prunes, peaches, pears, plums, peas (P foods!) twice a day.
- Avoid constipating foods like applesauce, bananas, and baby cereal.
- Glycerin suppository (over-the-counter) with pediatrician approval.
- Seek pediatrician care if this is a reoccurring problem.

Diarrhea

Diarrhea is considered more than five watery stools within twenty-four hours. It may be difficult to tell if infant is urinating when they are having diarrhea, especially because they typically urinate when they have bowel movements. Check diaper very frequently to try to monitor if infant is urinating.

Under three months of age: contact pediatrician if persistent diarrhea occurs as newborns can become dehydrated quickly.

Over three months of age: monitor the frequency of wet and dirty diapers. If there has been no wet diaper in four to six hours and baby is not taking any fluids, contact pediatrician.

Things You Can Try for Diarrhea:
- Continue feeding as normal if they are tolerating it. If baby is eating solids, stick to starchy solids (e.g., cereal, crackers, applesauce, bananas, mashed potatoes)
- Ask your pediatrician about electrolyte drinks to prevent dehydration
- Change diapers frequently to prevent skin breakdown
- Use diaper rash cream preventatively, and see diaper rash section for more tips.

Signs to Call Pediatrician:
- Watery stools for longer than two days
- Blood or mucous in stool
- Fever
- Abdomen hard and tender at rest (not crying or pushing)
- Any signs of dehydration (no wet diapers in four to six hours, inside of lips are dry and tacky, no tears when crying, lethargy)

Vomiting

Large amounts of fluid being forcefully expelled, more than two to three times.

Under three months of age: contact pediatrician if persistent vomiting occurs as newborns can become dehydrated quickly.

Over three months of age: monitor the frequency of wet and dirty diapers. If there has been no wet diaper in four to six hours and baby is not taking any fluids, contact pediatrician.

Things You Can Try for Vomiting:

After vomiting, wait at least thirty minutes to offer fluids:

- If baby is fed breastmilk, you can continue to attempt to feed breastmilk in small quantities.
- If baby is formula fed or not tolerating breastmilk, you can try one teaspoon of clear liquids (water, electrolyte drink) every ten minutes or so if they are keeping it down. If baby tolerates this, you can keep trying small amounts of fluids every ten to fifteen minutes. Slowly increase amount of clear liquids.
- You can use a spoon, syringe, or bottle to offer these small amounts of liquid.
- Baby can suck on popsicles (use popsicle molds or mesh teethers with frozen water or electrolyte drink if baby hasn't had solids yet).
- If no vomiting in eight hours, you can attempt to return to breastfeeding/formula.
- If baby vomits again at any point, start back with a teaspoon amount and work your way back up.
- If baby has a fever as well and cannot tolerate oral medications, you could ask your pediatrician about an acetaminophen suppository.
- If infant is old enough to eat solids, they likely will not have an appetite for solids. Just focus on keeping them hydrated with fluids.

- Once they are able to tolerate solids again, start with simple carbs such as bread, crackers, applesauce, or bananas.

Things You Can Try to Contain the Mess:

- Line whatever furniture you are using for baby (couch/crib/bed) with absorbent pads (puppy training pads), a mattress protector, or towels.
- You can use the same things on the floor next to the furniture, or use shower liners.
- Infants typically cannot manage to throw up into a receptacle; using disposable absorbent pads or hand towels to catch the vomit could be an option.
- If they are able to throw up into a bowl/small garbage can, line it with grocery bags or small garbage bags to make clean-up easier!

Signs to Call Pediatrician:

- Vomiting blood or bile (fluorescent yellow or green goo)
- Vomiting with full-body rash
- Fever
- Abdomen hard and tender at rest (not crying or pushing)
- Blood in stool
- Signs of dehydration (no wet diapers in four to six hours, inside of lips are dry and tacky, no tears when crying, lethargy)

Diaper Rash

Prevention:

Change baby's diaper frequently, use barrier cream, and avoid acidic or irritating foods.

Things You Can Try for Diaper Rash:

- Diaper rash creams—either petroleum jelly or creams that contain zinc oxide. This may require trial and error to find which product works best for your baby.
- Open diaper time (on a towel if baby is non-mobile) to let skin get air flow.
- *Nona's Tip: If baby is mobile and going diaper-less is a risk you're not willing to take due to slips or messes, you can try cutting the elastic band off either side of the diaper, with caution not to cut into the absorption pad. This will allow airflow to pass through to baby's skin while catching most of the mess.*
- Instead of using a wet wipe to clean stool off of baby's butt, try using saline spray, or a spray bottle of warm water (your post-partum peri bottle would work great!) to loosen the stool. Use soft wash cloths to dab the skin when cleaning; don't rub.
- A lot of baby wipes have fragrance in them that can further irritate the skin, even if they aren't specified on front of packaging. Make sure to read the ingredients.
- Baths with baking soda or breast milk may help sooth the area and help the skin heal faster.
- If diaper rash becomes red and bumpy, it may have turned into a fungal rash. Your pediatrician could prescribe an antifungal cream for this!
- Acidic foods or too much juice can cause diaper rashes; try watering juice down if this is a concern.

Thrush

White patches on baby's tongue, gums, or cheeks that do not come off when wiped with a cloth. Thrush is caused by a yeast and is made worse by friction from too much time sucking on pacifier.

When to Call Pediatrician:

- Baby is difficult to feed, or unable to bottle/nurse due to discomfort in the mouth
- Baby develops fever
- You notice a thrush infection on your nipples (if breastfeeding)

Things You Can Try for Thrush:

- Antifungal medicine is applied directly to thrush infection with a cloth/swab
- Sterilizing bottles/pacifiers/breastfeeding supplies or anything your baby mouths on frequently
- Wipe out baby's mouth with a wet cloth after feeds to prevent formula residue from sitting in mouth
- Treat your nipples with antifungal medicine if breastfeeding
- Limit pacifier use to prevent further irritation in mouth

Miscellaneous Information

- Babies should not consume honey until they are at least one year old.
- No sunscreen until six months old. Once they are six months old, be sure to use it even when weather is overcast. Do not use spray sunscreen on babies.
- Girls can have vaginal discharge after being born.
- Boys that are circumcised: Once the skin is healed enough to stop using petroleum jelly, you should retract the foreskin a few times a day to prevent penile adhesions from forming. They can occur months after the circumcision.
- Safe sleeping is laying on their back with no blankets, pillows, or stuffed animals until twelve months.
- No more arm swaddling once baby learns to roll over.
- Babies feed off your emotions; if you're tense and upset, baby will be too.
- You should be sterilizing your baby's bottles until at least two months of age.
- Trimming your baby's nails when they are asleep or drowsy can make it fuss-free. Cutting them after a bath makes the nails softer and easier to cut.
- You can size up diapers at nighttime to prevent urine leaks once your baby starts giving you longer stretches of sleep at night.
- Poison Control Center #800-222-1222

I encourage readers to cut out the following pages or create your own with empty tables to fill out with the correct weight-based dosing based off the medication kept in your home. Keep on your fridge or in a spot near your medicine cabinet for an easy reference for all caregivers.

Medication Dosing

Medicine Name	Weight	Dose in mL

I encourage readers to cut out the following pages or create your own with empty tables to fill out with the correct weight-based dosing based off the medication kept in your home. Keep on your fridge or in a spot near your medicine cabinet for an easy reference for all caregivers.

Medication Schedule

Medicine Name	Dose in mL	Time Given

Recommended Resources

https://www.aap.org

https://www.healthychildren.org

https://www.cdc.gov

https://www.nichd.nih.gov/health/topics/infantcare

https://www.nlm.nih.gov

https://llli.org

References

Gardner SL, Carter BS, Enzman-Hines M, Niermeyer S, eds. Merenstein & Gardner's Handbook of Neonatal Intensive Care: An Interprofessional Approach. 9th ed. Elsevier; 2021.

Anderson CE, Herring RA. Pediatric nursing interventions and skills. In: Hockenberry MJ, Wilson D, Rodgers CC, eds. Wong's Nursing Care of Infants and Children. 11th ed. e-Book. Elsevier; 2019.

Patient Safety Network. Medication administration errors. Agency for Healthcare Research and Quality. Updated March 2021. https://psnet.ahrq.gov

Alibrahim O, Slain K. Noninvasive ventilation in the pediatric intensive care unit. In: Zimmerman JJ, Clark RSB, Fuhrman BP, Rotta AT, Kudchadkar SR, eds. *Fuhrman & Zimmerman's Pediatric Critical Care*. 6th ed. Elsevier; 2022.

Skin-to-skin care. La Leche League International. October 13, 2019.

Garzon Maaks DL, Barber Starr N, Brady MA, Gaylord NM, Driessnack M, Duderstadt KG, eds. Burns' Pediatric Primary Care. 7th ed. Elsevier; 2020.

National Association of Neonatal Nurses (NANN). Policies, procedures, and competencies for neonatal nursing care. 6th ed. NANN; 2019.

Trisha Korioth; Doses done right: Read labels before giving pain medicine to children. *AAP News* April 2014; 35 (4): 26. 10.1542/aapnews.2014354-26d

Acetaminophen Dosing Tables for Fever and Pain in Children. American Academy of Pediatrics Council on Quality Improvement and Patient Safety. October 2021. Retrieved from: https://www.healthychildren.org/English/safety-prevention/at-home/medication-safety/Pages/Acetaminophen-for-Fever-and-Pain.aspx

Ibuprofen Dosing Table for Fever and Pain. American Academy of Pediatrics Council on Quality Improvement and Patient Safety. September 2024. Retrieved from https://www.healthychildren.org/English/safety-prevention/at-home/medication-safety/Pages/Ibuprofen-for-Fever-and-Pain.aspx?_gl=1*mre81n*_ga*MzYzMTgwNTgwLjE3MzQxMDc1NTU.*_ga_F D9D3XZVQQ*MTczNDEwNzU1NS4xLjEuMTczNDEwNzc5MC4wLjAuMA..

How to Take your Child's Temperature. American Academy of Pediatrics.A April 2024. Retrieved from: https://www.healthychildren.org/English/health-issues/conditions/fever/Pages/How-to-Take-a-Childs-Temperature.aspx

Diphenhydramine Dosing Table. American Academy of Pediatrics Council on Quality Improvement and Patient Safety. October 2021. Retrieved from: https://www.healthychildren.org/English/safety-prevention/at-home/medication-safety/Pages/Diphenhydramine-Benadryl-Antihistamine.aspx?_gl=1*u4soah*_ga*MzYzMTgwNTgwLjE3MzQxMDc1NTU.*_ga_FD9D3X ZVQQ*MTczNDEwNzU1NS4xLjEuMTczNDEwNzgyMi44wLjAuMA..

Lorenzo C. Patient education: Nausea and vomiting in infants and children. November 2024. Accessed December 2024.

De Luca A, Zanelli G. Gastroenteritis and Intractable Diarrhea in Newborns. Neonatology. 2018 May 8:1355–63. doi: 10.1007/978-3-319-29489-6_233. PMCID: PMC7123415.

McFadden H. Parental concerns on gastroesophageal reflux. Clinical Lactation. Jan 2017. Volume 8 Issue 4. DOI: 10.1891/2158-0782.8.4.169

Horii K. Patient education: Diaper rash in infants and children (Beyond the Basics). UpToDate. Feb 2024. Retrieved from: https://www.uptodate.com/contents/diaper-rash-in-infants-and-children-beyond-the-basics/print

www.ingramcontent.com/pod-product-compliance
Lightning Source LLC
Chambersburg PA
CBHW051651120626
46551CB00015B/2315